Published by
**Maple Tree Press Inc.**
51 Front Street East, Suite 200, Toronto, Ontario M5E 1B3
www.mapletreepress.com

Distributed in Canada by Raincoast Books
9050 Shaughnessy Street, Vancouver, British Columbia V6P 6E5

Distributed in the United States by Publishers Group West
1700 Fourth Street, Berkeley, California 94710

We acknowledge the financial support of the Canada Council for the Arts, the Government
of Canada through the Book Publishing Industry Development Program (BPIDP), the
Government of Ontario through the Ontario Media Development Corporation's Book
Initiative, and the Ontario Arts Council for our publishing activities.

ONTARIO ARTS COUNCIL
CONSEIL DES ARTS DE L'ONTARIO

## Dedication
*To all of our daughters and the mothers
who brought them into our world*

Cataloguing in Publication Data
Wallace, Mary, 1950-
    The girls' spa book : 20 dreamy ways to relax and feel great / Mary Wallace, Jessica Wallace ;
illustrated by Claudia Dávila.

(Girl zone)
Includes index.
ISBN 1-897066-00-7 (bound).     ISBN 1-897066-01-5 (pbk.)

1. Cosmetics—Juvenile literature.  2. Handicraft for girls—Juvenile literature. 3. Gifts—Juvenile literature.
I. Dávila, Claudia  II. Wallace, Jessica, 1978-  III. Title.  IV. Series.

RA777.25.W34 2003      j646.7'2   C2002-904071-X

**Design & Art Direction:** Claudia Dávila
**Illustrations:** Claudia Dávila
**Photography:** Mary Wallace

Printed in Belgium

A    B    C    D    E    F

# THE GIRLS' Spa BOOK

## 20 Dreamy Ways to Relax and Feel Great

**Written by Mary Wallace and Jessica Wallace**

**Photography by Mary Wallace**

**Illustrations by Claudia Dávila**

MAPLE TREE PRESS

# CONTENTS

## Getting Started

Looking Good, Feeling Great! 4
My Own Logo 6

## Materials

Ingredients 8
Tools & Containers 10
Color & Fragrance 12

## Recipes

Symbolic Body Art 14
Bath Soaking Salts 16
Bath Sizzlers 18
Bubbly Bath 20
Soapy Shower Gel 22
Soothing Body Scrub 24
Scented Bath Powder 26
Lovely Body Lotion 28
Luscious Lip Gloss 30
Dream Hand Cream 32
Sumptuous Shampoo 34
Herbal Hair Rinse 36
Foaming Face Wash 38
Fancy Foot Scrub 40
Candles of Light 42

## The Spirit of Sharing

My Label 44
Shapes & Symbols 46
The Meaning of Color 48
From Me to You 50
Just Relax 52
Card Collection 54
Magnificent Messages 56
Gift Boxes & Baskets 58
Your Gifts 60

## Endings

More on Girls' Spa 62
Acknowledgments 63
Index 64

# LOOKING GOOD, FEELING GREAT!

**Each of us is born a brilliantly unique person** with a special spark that is ours alone. We are at our best when we stay true to this wonderful part of ourselves.

The world today is an exciting and interesting place, and life can get very busy. At times you probably feel as if too much is going on and you're being pulled in too many different directions. When this happens, you might lose focus of who the real you is. That means it's time to take a break and *stress less*!

This book is filled with fun ways to relax, de-stress, feel great about yourself, and celebrate the person you are. Making sensational spa products will help you find ways to enjoy your unique mind, body, and spirit. In the section "The Spirit of Sharing" you'll find ideas for sharing those personal gifts with friends and family.

Throughout this book, look for Girl Talks like the one below to see what other girls have to say about finding and caring for their own inner strength and beauty.

Feel beautiful both inside and out. Let your light shine!

## Girl Talk

"Beauty comes from within, and radiates outwards to touch others." Natalie

# MY OWN LOGO

**Beauty is more than skin deep.** It's about the inner glow that shines from a person who feels good about who she is. Can you feel that special spark within yourself? What do you imagine it looks like?

Design a logo that expresses something about that mysterious part of yourself. Your logo will be a symbol that celebrates who you are. You can use it on anything you create, including labels for the products you make from recipes in this book (see page 44).

## You'll Need
• paper
• colored pencils or crayons

**1** Gather your materials and find a quiet space to work.

**2** Draw a large circle on your paper.

**3** Put your name in the center.

**4** Write " I am…", "I can…", and "I feel…" around the circle's edge, filling in thoughts, actions, and feelings to complete each sentence.

**5** As you think good things about yourself, imagine simple shapes, colors, or symbols that express what you mean. For ideas, look at the pages on shapes and symbols and color (see pages 46 to 49).

**6** Draw these images around your circle.

Girl Talk

*"I am just me. I hope that's ok. I don't want to change, I like me this way."* Megan

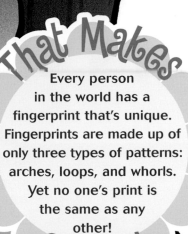

Jessica's logo

I am strong

I can make things happen

Jessica

I feel light and joyful

You might choose the symbol of a leaf because
you feel that, like a plant, you have grown a lot lately.
And you may color it red because of your fiery energy.
For more on symbols, color, and meaning, see pages 46 to 49.

# INGREDIENTS

See pages 13 and 36.

### Almond Extract

**Warning**
Do not use almond extract or oil if you have a nut allergy.

An oil made from almond nuts, used as both a food flavor and a fragrant scent.

### Almond or Canola Oil

A pale, almost odorless oil is made from the almond nut. You can also use a light oil such as canola oil.

### Baby Shampoo or Liquid Soap

A mild shampoo with few additives or perfumes. You can substitute a mild liquid soap.

### Cocoa Butter

A soft waxy oil made from the roasted seeds of the cocoa plant (which also gives us chocolate!).

### Cornstarch

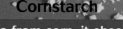

Made from corn, it absorbs moisture and helps soothe and relieve itchy and dry skin.

### Epsom Salts

A mineral salt, also called magnesium sulfate.

### Herbs

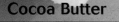

See pages 13 and 36.

### Honey

Made by bees from nectar collected from flowers; a natural antibacterial agent.

### Lemon Extract

An oil made from the peel of the lemon, used both as a food flavor and as a fragrant scent.

### Rose Water

A natural flower fragrance made from dried rose petals.

### Sand

Fine granulated rock, found on the seashore, riverbeds, and deserts.

### Sea Salt

From evaporated ocean water; used as a preservative (you can substitute table salt).

# All of the ingredients used in the recipes in this

book are fairly inexpensive, are non-toxic when used as recommended, and are available at your local grocery, health, or drugstore. Some might even come from a home garden. Since the ingredients suggested here are natural, not synthetic, you will probably find that the products you make are kind to you and your skin.

**Do not taste or eat any of the ingredients.**

**Beeswax**

From the honeycomb bees build. Get it from a beekeeper, health food store, or arts and crafts store.

**Baking Soda**

A non-toxic, weak acidic powder. Combined with certain ingredients, it "fizzes" on contact with water.

**Citric Acid**

This non-toxic acid acts as a preservative, and can be found in the grocery store.

**Food Color**

Certified safe, but use only a drop or two; more will temporarily dye skin and sinks.

**Gelatin**

Derived from animal protein; it acts as a thickener.

**Glycerin**

A heavy, sticky liquid that's a natural by-product of soap manufacturing.

**Olive oil**

A pale yellow oil made from ripe olives.

**Peppermint Extract**

An oil made from mint plants, used both as a food flavor and as a fragrant scent.

**Petroleum Jelly**

A lubricant obtained from the refining of crude oils.

**Vanilla**

An oil made from the vanilla bean, used both as a food flavor and as a fragrant scent.

**Witch Hazel**

A soothing, mild astringent made from the twigs of the alder bush.

**Test Patches**

Some ingredients might cause an allergic reaction. If you're not sure, test the product. Apply a bit to a patch of skin in the inside crease of your elbow. Leave on several hours or overnight. A red, itchy, or swollen spot might mean you're allergic to an ingredient in the product.

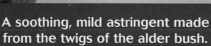

# TOOLS & CONTAINERS

## Use these kitchen tools to measure and mix your ingredients:

**You'll Need**
- microwavable measuring cup
- microwave oven
- measuring spoons
- funnel
- grater
- mixing spoon
- mixing bowl

Always use a microwave oven under the supervision of an adult. Never put metal (spoons, foil, etc.) in the microwave. Be careful when handling heated ingredients. Use oven mitts to protect your hands.

### Measuring
One spoon = 15 mL = 1 tablespoon (tbsp.) = 1 level soupspoon
One cup = 250 mL = 8 oz. = 1 mug

You'll also need a variety of containers to put your products into. Collect and reuse empty glass and plastic pots, jars, and bottles (from food, beverages, and cosmetics). Grocery stores, drugstores, and dollar stores are all good places to buy new containers, small and large. Each one should have a lid that screws or snaps on.

Glass and plastic containers have different uses; you will need some of each. Glass containers are breakable. They are best for products that can be scooped out (like bath salts and bath fizzies), so make sure they have wide openings. Plastic containers are not as likely to break. Use them for products that are poured or squeezed out.

Store your filled containers with the lids tightly shut. Keep them in a cool, dark cupboard. If your product smells funny or becomes discolored over time, throw it out; it may no longer be safe to use.

How to clean your containers:

**1** Rinse to remove leftover food, cosmetics, etc. Soak to remove labels.

**2** Wash well in hot, soapy water.

**3** Rinse with clean water and dry.

# COLOR & FRAGRANCE

**You can add subtle hints** of color to the products you make. Most ingredients in the recipes are white, so you will need to add only a few drops of color (no more than five drops) to create a pastel hue. If you add too much color, you will end up temporarily dyeing your skin and the tub, sink, or shower. See page 48 for information on the meanings of colors.

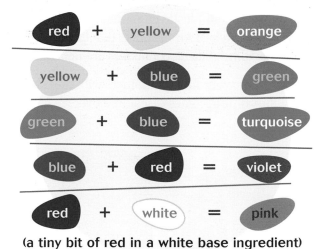

red + yellow = orange

yellow + blue = green

green + blue = turquoise

blue + red = violet

red + white = pink

**(a tiny bit of red in a white base ingredient)**

## You'll Need

• Food coloring in three primary colors: yellow, blue, and red

**1** Mix colors (use just a few drops of each).

**2** Add your chosen color to a spoonful of one of the ingredients in a cup or bowl. Stir well.

**3** Add this mixture to the rest of the product. Stir until all the color is blended.

# Scented Sachets

**Smell is one of the most powerful** of your senses. You can add a touch of light fragrance to the products you make. An attractive smell will delight your senses—either relaxing or invigorating you.

To avoid allergic reactions, use small quantities of natural ingredients, as suggested in the product recipes. Food flavoring is a safe and effective additive that adds a lovely scent. Mix a few drops of almond, vanilla, lemon, or peppermint extract with a small amount of the ingredient first. Then mix this portion with the rest of the ingredients.

For dry products, use dried herbs from a garden or from herbal tea bags. You can make your own scented sachets to add fragrance to dry products.

### Warning
Do not use almond extract if you have a nut allergy.

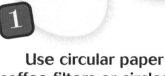

**1** Use circular paper coffee filters or circles of cheesecloth for sachets.

**2** Place dry ingredients in center of cloth or paper circle.

**3** Gather edges to close and fasten with a rubber band and ribbon.

**4** Place sachet in container, then pour product on top. Fasten lid so the scent will permeate through the product. This may take up to two weeks.

## That Makes Scents!

The gorgeous flowering vanilla plant grows as a climbing vine in tropical regions. It produces pods that look like very large beans. These are harvested so that the oils can be extracted for use in flavorings and fragrances.

## Girl Talk

"One of my best strengths is my ability to accept myself."
Elizabeth

# SYMBOLIC BODY ART

**Decorating your skin is a visual way** of expressing your thoughts and feelings. Various types of body art—including body jewelry, piercing, tattoos, and henna—have been used throughout history. Some body decoration alters the skin permanently, but in today's world of rapid change, temporary designs are popular.

Here's a safe and simple technique for wearing a personal design on your skin. Choose a symbol and color (see pages 46–49) that say something about you. Practice your design on paper first. A small design looks best. The right place for it might be just above your ankle, on your wrist, or on your upper arm.

To use more than one color, apply them one at a time and let dry between applications. Your colorful body art should not touch clothes or furniture until it is completely dry (takes a few minutes).

## You'll Need

- one drop of food color
- a small plate
- a small, fine-pointed paintbrush
- tissue
- a piece of paper
- bath powder, see page 26 (can substitute cornstarch)

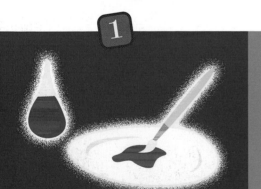

**1** Put a drop of food color onto the plate. Dip a dry brush tip into the food color and blot off excess with a tissue (too much color will make blurry edges).

**2** Practice drawing your design on paper. Keep your hand steady by bracing your wrist.

**3** Apply a small amount of powder to the place where you will be painting your design. Wipe off excess with a clean tissue (this helps to dry your skin so that the edges of your design won't blur).

# Girl Talk

Try body art with friends, planning and painting tiny designs for each other.

**4**

Paint your design onto your skin. If you don't like it, wash it off immediately with soap and water. Let dry.

## That Makes Scents!

Mehndi, or henna, is a reddish-brown dye made from the leaves of a bush that grows in the Middle East, Asia, and North Africa. For more than 5,000 years, it has been used in temporary tattoos that last anywhere from several days to several weeks. The hands of Ancient Persian brides and dancers were decorated with mehndi, as were the hands and feet of Indian princes and princesses. In South Asia today, mehndi decoration is important in preparing for a wedding, as friends and relatives spend an evening painting intricate line and dot designs, forming gorgeous "gloves" and "stockings" on the lucky bride-to-be.

15

# BATH SOAKING SALTS

**Yield**
Makes about
1 L (4 cups)

## Use bath time as a
time to think about things. Easy to make and fabulous to use, bath salts are a fantastic way to relax and refresh.

**1** Mix Epsom and sea salts with baking soda in bowl.

**2** Add food color and scent to small amount of mixture in measuring cup. Stir well.

**3** Combine all ingredients in bowl. Stir well.

**4** Pour or spoon mixture into jar (or jars). Try layering different colors. Use wide-mouthed jars so that if the mixture hardens, it will be easier to get out.

## You'll Need

- large mixing bowl
- mixing spoon
- measuring cup
- 625 mL (2 1/2 cups) Epsom salts
- 125 mL (1/2 cup) sea salt
- 250 mL (1 cup) baking soda
- food color (see page 12)
- food flavoring for fragrance (see pages 8–9 and 13)
- large, lidded wide-mouthed jar(s)

Add about 125 mL (1/2 cup) to your bath water. Or use 125 mL (1/2 cup) in a basin of warm water for a relaxing foot soak.

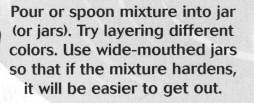

## Girl Talk

"If something is bothering me I go somewhere alone to think with nobody bothering me. Most often I have a bath and think about things." *Janelle*

That Makes Scents!

In many cultures, water is considered sacred. It is traditionally used in rituals to clean and purify the spirit.

### Shortcut

Mix Epsom salts with a bit of color and fragrance and pour into a small jar.

# BATH SIZZLERS

**Being true to yourself** is not always easy, but it does mean that your life can be full of sparkling, sizzling adventure. Celebrate yourself with these fun, fizzling, frothy bath beauties. They will add a delightful touch of liveliness to your soak.

## That Makes Scents!

Ancient Greeks believed that water was a health-giving gift from the gods. They enjoyed baths and showers at home, as well as hot sulfur spring baths, natural spring water baths, and steam baths.

## You'll Need

- mixing bowl
- mixing spoon
- measuring cup and measuring spoons
- 250 mL (1 cup) baking soda
- 45 mL (3 tbsp.) citric acid
- 45 mL (3 tbsp.) cornstarch
- 45 mL (3 tbsp.) light oil (almond or canola oil)
- food color (see page 12)
- food flavoring for fragrance (see pages 8–9 and 13)
- clear plastic wrap
- ribbon

**Warning**
Do not use almond oil if you have a nut allergy.

**1** Mix baking soda, citric acid, and cornstarch in bowl.

**2** Measure out oil, color, and scent. Stir.

**3** Add to bowl and mix well.

**Shortcut** Mix the baking soda, citric acid, and cornstarch in a jar.

18

After filling your tub with water, climb in, add two sizzlers and enjoy the fizzle.

# Girl Talk

"We all have stress in our lives, but it's important not to get overwhelmed. A good way to make sure this doesn't happen is to do at least one thing that you feel good about every day." Caitlin

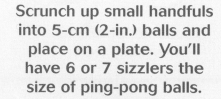

**4** Scrunch up small handfuls into 5-cm (2-in.) balls and place on a plate. You'll have 6 or 7 sizzlers the size of ping-pong balls.

**5** Let dry for two days.

**6** Wrap each ball separately in plastic wrap. Tie closed with ribbon in a small bow.

Sprinkle a few spoonfuls into your bathwater for instant sizzle.

# BUBBLY BATH

**There's nothing more fun** than a bathtub filled with bubbles. Hearing and feeling the tiny bubbles pop is relaxing. Playing and sculpting the soapy, sudsy layers is even more delightful.

**Yield** Makes about 250 mL (1 cup)

## You'll Need

- mixing bowl
- measuring cup and measuring spoons
- mixing spoon
- 170 mL (2/3 cup) water
- 85 mL (1/3 cup) baby shampoo or liquid soap
- 15 mL (1 tbsp.) glycerin
- food color (see page 12)
- food flavoring for fragrance (see pages 8–9 and 13)
- funnel
- plastic squeeze bottle

**1** Mix water, soap, and glycerin in bowl.

**2** Add color and fragrance. Stir.

**3** Ask someone to hold the funnel while you pour mixture into plastic squeeze bottle.

**4** Close lid. Shake to mix really well.

Squeeze a dollop under the tapwater while your bath is filling.

## That Makes Scents!

Deep breathing calms your body and mind. Lie down or sit comfortably with your hands resting on your lap, palms up. Gently and slowly breathe in through your nose to a count of four. Fill your lungs as full as possible and let your stomach expand out. Hold the breath in for a second or two. Then let your stomach relax as you slowly breathe out through your mouth to a count of six, exhaling until your lungs feel empty. Don't worry about whether you're doing it right or wrong, just focus on the sound and feel of your breath as you inhale and exhale.

## Girl Talk

"Just breathe and take a step back."

Salima

## More Bubbles!

Make some bubble juice for blowing bubbles while sitting in the tub. Mix 250 mL (1 cup) water with 30 mL (2 tbsp.) of glycerin and 125 mL (1/2 cup) of dishwashing liquid. Add a bit of food color and pour into a wide-mouthed plastic jar. Form a twist tie into a circle with a handle. Dip into the bubble juice and watch the bubbles you blow float down to join the ones in the water.

# SOAPY SHOWER GEL

**Yield**

Makes about
250 mL (1 cup)

## You'll Need

- microwavable measuring cup and measuring spoons
- mixing spoon
- mixing bowl
- 125 mL (1/2 cup) water
- 15 mL (1 tbsp.) unflavored gelatin
- food color (see page 12)
- food flavoring for fragrance (see pages 8–9 and 13)
- 125 mL (1/2 cup) baby shampoo or liquid soap
- funnel
- plastic squeeze bottle

## A morning shower helps you

wake up, stretch, and plan for the day. A shower in the evening is a time to relax and let all the worries of the day swirl down the drain. Here's a fun and easy way to make a refreshing shower gel.

**1** Mix water and gelatin in microwavable measuring cup.

**2** Heat in microwave for one minute on high.

**3** Stir. Be careful, it's hot.

**WARNING:** Ask an adult to help when you use the microwave. Your mixture will be HOT! Handle with oven mitts, caution, and adult supervision.

**4** Pour into bowl and add color, fragrance, and soap. Stir.

**5** Have someone hold the funnel while you pour into squeeze bottle. Refrigerate to set.

Squeeze a dollop onto your washcloth and scrub away.

Gentle stretching can relax tense muscles.

## Neck stretches

Tilt your head slowly from side to side, holding for ten seconds on each side. Then gently rotate your chin in a circle a couple of times.

## Arm stretches

Put your hands up over your head and reach as high as is comfortable. Hold for a few seconds. Reach over your head with your right arm and move it toward your left shoulder. Now return your right arm slowly, and repeat the process with your left arm, moving it toward your right shoulder.

## Shoulder stretches

Lift your shoulders toward your ears for ten seconds. Then release and relax your shoulders; try this three or four times. Next, slowly rotate your shoulders in circles forward, then backward.

Girl Talk

"When I come out of the shower, I look into the steamy mirror and trace my face. As I draw with my finger, my reflection becomes clearer. I like to make different faces and trace them beside, over, and under each other to create a collage of moods." Jan

# Soothing BODY SCRUB

**Yield** Makes one soothing body scrub for one-time use

## Do you get irritated or angry when someone or

something is really bugging you? There are all sorts of ways to get rid of your frustration and anger without taking it out on another person—or yourself! Soothe or invigorate yourself as needed with this traditional oatmeal body scrub. It will soften your skin as well as your temper.

### You'll Need
- measuring cup
- washcloth
- 250 mL (1 cup) oatmeal
- rubber band
- ribbon

*Girl Talk* "I handle stress by crying. It always makes me feel better because I let everything out." **Erin**

**1**
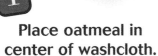
**Place oatmeal in center of washcloth.**

**2**
**Gather edges and fasten with rubber band.**

**3**

**Place ribbon over rubber band and tie.**

Use in the shower or tub for a facial or whole body treat. Wet the washcloth and rub it gently on your skin. Squeeze it to release the soothing creamy oatmeal. After use, undo the ribbon and rubber band to remove damp oatmeal (which you can compost).

# Make a Shower Scrubby

A scrubbing sponge is easy to make and invigorating to use. A scrubby not only cleans off dirt, it helps remove dead skin cells. A colorful scrubby makes a perfect accessory when you give a gift of shower gel or bubble bath.

**3** You will have 6 strips, each about 1 m (1 yd.) long and 16 cm (6 in.) wide.

**4** Place strips on top of each other. Gather the middle of your pile of strips along the length.

**1** Fold width of fabric in half. Cut along fold.

**2** Fold each half into thirds (lengthwise); cut along folds.

**5** Hold the bunched fabric while a friend places ribbon around the middle, tying with one simple overhand knot. Pull tight to gather. Knot several times to hold in place.

**6** Tie ends of ribbon to form a handle.

Separate and adjust each layer of your scrubby—it will blossom like a flower. Use this in the shower or bath with a bit of soap or shower gel.

**Alternative** Make a heat bag to soothe tense muscles. Put 500 mL (2 cups) of dry rice, lentils, or dry beans in a tube sock. Tie it tightly shut. Microwave on high for two minutes and place on your sore muscles.

# Scented BATH POWDER

**Yield**

Makes about
185 mL (3/4 cup)

## When it comes to being happy and successful,

attitude is much more important than ability. Remember that your life will be what you make of it, what you think of it, and what you want it to be.

Enjoy simple pleasures and be grateful for small things. Take delight in the lovely smell and feel of this silky after-bath powder.

## You'll Need

- mixing bowl
- mixing spoon
- measuring cup
- 125 mL (1/2 cup) cornstarch
- 60 mL (1/4 cup) baking soda

- fragrant herb sachet (see page 13)
- wide-mouthed jar with lid
- powder puff* or small, soft sponge

*Buy at your local drugstore or cosmetics counter.

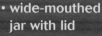

# That Makes Scents!

Optimistic people are happier, healthier, and more successful than those with a negative outlook on life. People who have a more positive attitude expect great things, work hard for those things, and are more likely to achieve them.

## Girl Talk

"Happiness is the euphoric feeling you experience when all is well in your world and nothing can wipe the gigantic smile off your ecstatic face and no one can put out the shining light in your twinkling eyes." Meg

Decide to be someone who dreams of wonderful things and expects to live out those dreams.

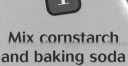

**1** Mix cornstarch and baking soda in bowl.

**2** Place fragrant sachet in bottom of wide-mouthed jar.

**3** Spoon mixture on top of sachet.

**4** Wait a week or two before use, so the powder has time to absorb the scent.

Towel yourself dry after a bath or shower and lightly feather bath powder onto your body using a powder puff.

# Lovely BODY LOTION

**Yield**

Makes about 165 mL
(²/₃ cup)

**No matter how much you grow,** you have to stay comfortable in your own skin. This body lotion will leave it feeling soft and supple. The light, rich fragrance of the rose water makes smoothing on this lotion a treat.

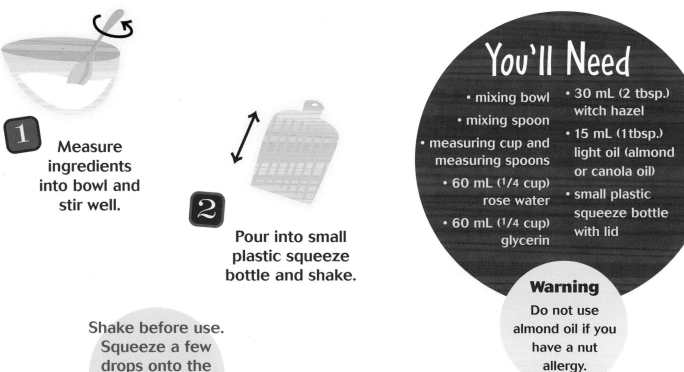

**1** Measure ingredients into bowl and stir well.

**2** Pour into small plastic squeeze bottle and shake.

Shake before use. Squeeze a few drops onto the palm of one hand and gently rub into your skin.

## You'll Need

- mixing bowl
- mixing spoon
- measuring cup and measuring spoons
- 60 mL (¹/₄ cup) rose water
- 60 mL (¹/₄ cup) glycerin
- 30 mL (2 tbsp.) witch hazel
- 15 mL (1 tbsp.) light oil (almond or canola oil)
- small plastic squeeze bottle with lid

**Warning**

Do not use almond oil if you have a nut allergy.

Girl Talk

"Even though Helen Keller couldn't see or hear, she was extraordinary. I try to remember what she said: 'The best and most beautiful things in the world cannot be seen or even touched. They must be felt with the heart.'" Katherine

## That Makes Scents!

Exposure to strong, admirable women can have protective and positive effects on girls. Girls who have a female role model to look up to are more likely to achieve their own goals—they have personally seen a woman succeed and know that they can too!

# Luscious LIP GLOSS

**You use your mouth** to share your ideas, thoughts, and feelings.

Be a good friend to yourself as well as others by being a good communicator, one who says positive things about yourself and others. Use this soft and smooth lip gloss to keep your lips in good shape.

## That Makes Scents!

Pretty + Popular does NOT = Perfect Happiness. Happiness comes from deeper within yourself.

## You'll Need

- grater
- microwavable measuring cup and measuring spoons
- mixing spoon
- mixing bowl
- 15 mL (1 tbsp.) beeswax
- 45 mL (3 tbsp.) light oil (almond or canola oil)
- food color (see page 12)
- food flavoring (a few drops of vanilla, lemon, peppermint, or almond extract, see pages 8–9)
- 250 mL (1 cup) cold water
- small lidded jar

### Warning

Do not use almond oil or almond extract if you have a nut allergy.

---

**1**

Grate a chunk of beeswax to make 15 mL (1 rounded tbsp.) of grated wax.

**2**

Place beeswax in microwavable measuring cup and add 15 mL (1 tbsp.) of the light oil.

**3**

Microwave on high for one minute. Stir to dissolve beeswax. (Your mixture should be clear.) WARNING: Ask an adult to help when you use the microwave. Your mixture will be HOT! Handle with oven mitts, caution, and adult supervision.

**4**

If mixture is not yet clear, microwave for thirty seconds. (Temperature of some microwaves may vary.) Stir.

"When I hear love songs on the radio, I dedicate them to myself instead of to someone else and then I sing along as loud as I can." Joan

**Pick up a bit of the lip gloss with the tip of your clean finger and smooth across your lips.**

**Shortcut** For a quick and easy lip gloss, mix 15 mL (1 tbsp.) of petroleum jelly with a few drops of food color and a few drops of food flavoring. Store it in a tiny jar or fill an empty lip gloss cylinder after you've washed it out.

 **5**

Add remaining 30 mL (2 tbsp.) oil. Stir until smooth. Add three drops of flavoring and one to five drops of coloring, for the depth of color you'd like. Stir.

 **6**

Pour 250 mL (1 cup) cold water into mixing bowl and place the cup of warm lip-gloss mixture into bowl.

**7**

Stir continuously to avoid lumps. As the mixture cools it will become thick and creamy. Be patient. It will take several minutes for it to mix, thicken, and color.

 **8**

Spoon into small lidded jar.

# DREAM
# HAND CREAM

**Yield**

Makes 180 mL (about 3/4 cup)

**Your hands are the tools** you use every day to take care of yourself, to draw and write about your world, to present a gift to yourself or to another, to extend in a gesture of friendship. Take good care of them.

## Girl Talk

"Friendship is having someone to confide in and trust. Friendship is like breathing, without it you would die."

Janelle

## You'll Need

- grater
- microwavable measuring cup and measuring spoons
- mixing spoon
- 60 mL (1/4 cup) beeswax
- 60 mL (1/4 cup) cocoa butter
- 60 mL (1/4 cup) olive oil
- small wide-mouthed jar with lid

Scoop out a small dab with your fingers and smooth onto your hands using soft and gentle strokes.

**1**

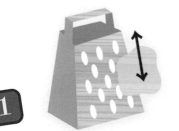

Grate a chunk of beeswax to make 60 mL (1/4 cup) of grated wax.

**2**

Place in microwavable measuring cup and add 15 mL (1 tbsp.) of the cocoa butter. Microwave on high for one and a half minutes. Stir to dissolve beeswax (your mixture should be clear).

**3**

Add rest of cocoa butter. Microwave for one more minute. Stir until smooth.

**WARNING:** Ask an adult to help when you use the microwave. Your mixture will be HOT! Handle with oven mitts, caution, and adult supervision.

**4**

If mixture is not yet clear, microwave for thirty seconds. (Temperature of microwaves may vary.) Stir.

**5**

Add olive oil and stir until creamy and smooth. Be patient. This will take several minutes.

**6**

Spoon into jar. Let harden.

33

# SUMPTUOUS SHAMPOO

**Yield**

Makes about 270 mL (a little more than 1 cup)

## Your hair may be thick, thin, or in-between.

It might be long or short, straight, curly, frizzy, and almost any color of the rainbow. One of the ways you express your uniqueness is the way you wear your hair.

This shampoo is a gentle alternative to commercial shampoos, conditioning your hair as it cleans. And it smells delicious, too.

## Girl Talk

"You don't have to be somebody different, you are just yourself."

Sarah

## You'll Need

- mixing bowl
- measuring cup and measuring spoons
- mixing spoon
- 15 mL (1 tbsp.) unflavored gelatin
- 250 mL (1 cup) baby shampoo or liquid soap
- a pinch of table salt
- 15 mL (1 tbsp.) light oil (almond oil or canola oil)
- a few drops of vanilla, lemon, peppermint, or almond extract
- a drop of food coloring (optional)
- funnel
- large plastic squeeze bottle

### Warning

Do not use almond oil or almond extract if you have a nut allergy.

**1** In mixing bowl, mix gelatin with 15 mL (1 tbsp.) of the baby shampoo.

**2** Measure remaining ingredients into the mixing bowl and stir well.

**3** Pour into squeeze bottle (have a friend hold the funnel as you pour).

## That Makes

How fast your hair grows depends on your age and on how long your hair already is. Hair grows fastest for women in their late teens and early twenties. If your hair is short, it will grow up to 0.5 cm (1/4 in.) every week. When it's long, it will grow only 0.25 cm (1/8 in.) every week.

## Scents!

Squeeze a quarter-sized dollop onto the palm of your hand. Rub your hands together; then gently work shampoo into your wet scalp and hair. Rinse thoroughly and gently towel dry.

# Herbal HAIR RINSE

**Yield** Makes 250 mL (1 cup)

**These hair rinses will leave your hair** clean, silky, and softly scented. Choose one that best suits your mood and your hair. They are safe to use as often as you like. Here are some herbs you can use to make rinses for your hair (all available from a grocery store or a home herb garden):

| |  |  |
|---|---|---|
| | **Catnip** | Some believe it will energize your hair and help it grow faster. |
| | **Chamomile** | Great for your scalp, it helps your hair grow shiny and healthy; brightens blond and red hair. |
| | **Lemon Balm** | Leaves your hair with a fresh citrus fragrance. (Or use lemon juice as a rinse to highlight blond hair.) |
| | **Parsley** | Relieves itchy scalp. |
| | **Rosemary** | Enriches the color of dark hair; will help control dandruff. |
| | **Sage** | Supercleans oily hair; helps heal damaged hair. |

**1** Place herbal tea bag or sachet in microwavable measuring cup; add water

**2** Microwave two minutes on high.

**WARNING:** Ask an adult to help when you use the microwave. Your mixture will be HOT! Handle with oven mitts, caution, and adult supervision.

**3** Let sit until cool.

**4** Stir, remove sachet, and pour rinse into plastic squeeze bottle.

• herb sachet (see page 13) or herbal tea bag

## You'll Need

- microwavable measuring cup
- spoon
- herb sachet (see page 13) or herbal tea bag
- 250 mL (1 cup) water
- plastic squeeze bottle

Squeeze herbal rinse onto your washed and still wet hair. Gently work into hair and leave it for five minutes. Lightly rinse with clean water. (Leave lemon or chamomile in your hair for a soft scent.) Air drying your hair will keep it healthier. Refrigerate leftover rinse in container with closed lid to prevent spoiling.

## That Makes Scents!

People have been changing and arranging their hair since prehistoric times. What hasn't changed is that we all have a natural hairstyle. Each of the more than 100,000 hairs on your head grows from a hair follicle that has a particular inborn shape. If you have round hair follicles, your hair will be naturally straight. If your follicles are oval, your hair will be wavy. And if you have curved hair follicles, your hair will be curly.

## Girl Talk

"A girl with self-esteem looks like she believes in herself."
Bobbi

# FOAMING FACE WASH

## Yield

Makes about 355 mL
(almost 1 ½ cups)

## Your face is the most expressive

part of your body. Subtle movements of your eyes, eyebrows, mouth, and cheek muscles show how you feel. Be kind to your face. Here's a recipe for a foaming face wash that will gently clean as it moisturizes your skin.

**That Makes**

Placing thin slices of cucumber over your eyes while you rest will help to cool and soothe tired or puffy skin.

**Scents!**

**1** Measure the honey and water in a microwavable measuring cup.

**2** Microwave on high for one minute. Stir.

**WARNING:** Ask an adult to help when you use the microwave. Your mixture will be HOT! Handle with oven mitts, caution, and adult supervision.

## You'll Need

- microwavable measuring cup and measuring spoons
- mixing bowl
- 30 mL (2 tbsp.) liquid honey
- 170 mL (2/3 cup) water
- pinch of salt
- 125 mL (1/2 cup) baby shampoo or liquid soap
- 30 mL (2 tbsp.) rose water
- drop of food color (optional)
- funnel
- plastic squeeze bottle

**3** Add remaining ingredients. Stir well.

**4** Pour into plastic squeeze bottle (have a friend hold the funnel).

Squeeze a quarter-sized dollop onto a clean, wet face cloth and gently scrub your face in small circular motions. Rinse well with clean water.

## Girl Talk

"When I am feeling great, anyone who sees me will know it—the smile on my face says it all. I try to share the great feelings with others, because smiles are contagious!

Natalie

# FANCY FOOT SCRUB

## You'll Need

- mixing bowl
- mixing spoon
- measuring cup and measuring spoons
- 15 mL (1 tbsp.) clean sand
- 60 mL (1/4 cup) sea salt
- 120 mL (1/2 cup) Epsom salts
- 15 mL (1 tbsp.) light oil (almond oil or canola oil)
- 15 mL (1 tbsp.) baby shampoo or liquid soap
- small wide-mouthed jar with lid

**Warning**

Do not use almond oil if you have a nut allergy.

**Yield**

Makes about 185 mL (3/4 cup)

## Sometimes your feet feel tired and sore,

yet you usually don't pay a lot of attention to them. For a nice change, pamper yourself with some gentle foot care. After a relaxing foot soak, this foot scrub will soothe, smooth, and exfoliate the soles of your feet.

**1**

Measure sand, sea salt, and Epsom salts into mixing bowl. Mix well.

**2**

Measure oil and shampoo into measuring cup. Stir and add to mixture in bowl.

**3**

Stir well and store in a small pot or jar.

Soak your feet in warm water (you can add 125 mL [1/2 cup] of bath salts from the recipe on page 16) for five to ten minutes. Rinse and dry your feet. Apply foot scrub to the soles of your feet using your fingers or a small sponge. Gently rub in circular motions. Rinse and dry.

# Girl Talk

"A friend is a footstep that walks beside you, a shoulder to cry on, someone to confide in, smiles, happiness, hugs, someone to lift your spirits to the clouds, to hold your hand and be there for you. Most importantly, to know you and still love you." Erin

## That Makes Scents!

Your feet provide the supporting base for your body. They have fifty-two bones, twenty-eight of them in your toes. Two flexible arches, along with a thick layer of fatty tissue, work together to absorb the pressures and shocks of walking, running, and jumping.

# CANDLES OF LIGHT

**Include a candle** in your relaxation experience. A candle is a symbol of truth and light in the darkness. The flickering candle light is calming and inspiring, and beeswax has a light, sweet scent that is delicious.

## That Makes

A single candle lamp provided an Inuit igloo with light and heat during the twenty-four hour darkness of an Arctic winter. A twisted bit of moss was placed in seal oil contained in hollowed-out soapstone—lit, it kept the snow home warm and cozy. An atmosphere of cooperation and sharing prevailed inside the igloo.

## Scents!

**1**

Lay beeswax sheet on a piece of waxed paper.

**2**

Cut off top edge of beeswax sheet at an angle and discard.

**3**

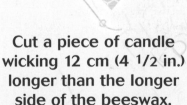

Cut a piece of candle wicking 12 cm (4 1/2 in.) longer than the longer side of the beeswax. Tie a knot at one end.

**4**

Place wick along longer edge of wax sheet (place knot at uncut edge).

**5**

Fold over a small edge of the side so that it lies over the wick. If the wax sheet is not flexible, warm with hair dryer.

**6**

Gently fold wax over again, then roll remainder of sheet around this folded edge.

**7**

Warm the base of the candle with hair dryer. Hold candle upright and press firmly against waxed paper surface to flatten base.

Place candle in a fireproof candle holder. Use caution when lighting your candle (only near fireproof surfaces) and never leave the candle unattended.

# MY LABEL

**You'll want to design great-looking labels** for the products you create. These labels will tell something about you—the person who made them. And they can illustrate the mood, thought, or idea you want to call to mind when you use the products they are attached to.

These folded labels look like little cards, with space on the inside to list ingredients and tell how to use the product. Keep your labels large enough to fit the information you'll write on the inside.

## You'll Need

- cardweight paper
- scissors
- pencil and pen
- colored paper
- glue
- paper holepunch
- string or ribbon
- white candle (optional)

**1**

Make a template out of cardweight paper. Trace the template along the folded edge of your colored paper.

**2**

Cut out. Note that a simple shape and a good size for your label work best.

**3**

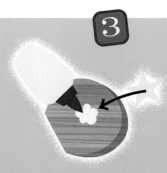

Choose one of the symbols from your logo (see pages 6 and 46). Draw it on colored paper and cut out. Glue onto front of label.

44

"Believe that your greatest beauty comes from inside. Let it show—you don't have to hide." Tallie

**Write ingredients and instructions for use on the inside. See each recipe page for this information.**

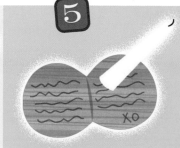

**(Optional) Waterproof the writing on your label by rubbing over it with a white candle, leaving a transparent wax coating that will help stop smears if your label gets wet.**

**Punch a hole through both "pages" of the label, making sure you don't punch out any writing. Thread with ribbon to attach to a container.**

**Repeat the process to make more labels. As you work, new ideas will occur to you, which you can incorporate into your label design.**

Spiral: creation, energy

Oval: new life, birth

Sun: cosmic power, brilliance

Moon: warmth, intuition

# SHAPES & SYMBOLS

Square: earth, integrity

Circle: wholeness, protection

Leaf: growth, health

Fire: energy, action

Water: dreams, mystery

Lightning: power, illumination

Air: flexibility, freedom

Earth: strength, grounding

Eye: insight, vision

Star: hope, loyalty

Butterfly: lightness, transformation

A symbol many people relate to is the image of an outstretched hand. Think about your reaction to seeing a hand reaching out to you. You would likely feel more warmth and friendliness than you would reading words describing a hand.

## Have you ever had an idea or feeling that couldn't be expressed using words alone? Pictures, drawings, and symbols can convey what words cannot. Symbols are simple drawings, used by humans to communicate since the beginning of time. Some symbols are universal, understood by people all over the world. For example, stars have been used for thousands of years to express hope and loyalty.

On these pages you'll see some symbols you might use as you create your personal logo (see page 6), labels (page 44), and cards (pages 50 to 57). Each symbol conveys a mood, thought, or feeling. Although each person has her own particular reaction to any symbol, some of the most common meanings associated with these symbols are shown here.

Candle: truth, light in the darkness

Hand: action, friendship

Girl Talk

"I'm the only one who can limit my possibilities." Kate

Heart: love, feeling

Rainbow: glory, wonder

Dewdrops: freshness, sparkling energy

Dove: peace

# THE MEANING OF COLOR

**We all have our favorite colors.** We know which colors make us feel good, and which we don't especially like. Think of the color of your favorite T-shirt and how it makes you feel. Now think of a color you would never wear and how it would make you feel if you had to wear it.

Throughout the ages, people have felt that color has an effect on the health and well-being of the body, mind, and spirit. Today, scientists are able to demonstrate the effects of exposure to different colors. Businesses are discovering that employees work better if surrounded by certain colors, and hospitals are becoming aware of the effects that colors have on their patients.

Use a variety of colors in the labels and cards you make, and even in the products you create using the recipes in this book. Choose colors that give you feelings and ideas that you'd like to communicate. For instance, white might speak to you of calmness, peacefulness, and purity. On the opposite page, you'll see some of the ways that people have interpreted the effects and meanings of color. (See page 12 for color mixing.)

## That Makes Scents!

Sunlight is a source of health and nourishment. When it passes through a prism, it separates into the colors of the spectrum: red, orange, yellow, green, blue, indigo, and violet—the colors in a rainbow.

## Girl Talk

"I love it when I can be creative and am free to do things my own way. I feel colorful when I am connected to nature, such as when I'm walking through the green woods, running under a blue sky, looking at the brilliant white stars, feeling the yellow sunshine, and watching the red sunset." Amber

Red – strength, joy, security

Orange – confidence, warmth, community

Yellow – clarity, wisdom, personal power

Green – growth, balance, healing

Turquoise – communication, truth, determination

Blue – understanding, truth, intuition

Violet – insight, beauty, creativity

Pink – love, friendship, caring

# FROM ME TO YOU

Natalie's Card

**A great way to enjoy the**
spa products you create is to share them with others. You can give them as gifts accompanied by handmade cards. As well as looking great, a card that you make will send an extra unspoken message that you cared enough to spend time and thought in its creation.

## That Makes Scents!

If you had a party in Ancient Egypt, you'd have presented your guests with wax cones of scented oil to wear on their heads. Through the evening, the wax melted and the oil covered the guests' hair and faces.

## Girl Talk

*"Friendship is loyal, selfless, trustworthy and comforting. Friendship is you."* Salima

# Create a Card

## You'll Need

- colored cardweight paper
- ruler
- pencil
- scissors
- glue
- colored paper from old magazines, calendars, wrapping paper, paper bags, etc.

**1**

Measure and mark halfway point on top and bottom of a piece of cardweight paper.

**2**

Following a ruler, press firmly with metal point of scissors to indent the line, making sure not to cut all the way through.

**3**

Fold paper over along scored edge.

**4**

Cut or tear side edge of front of the card to add texture.

**5**

The next few pages will give you ideas for creating designs and messages for your cards.

# Make an Envelope

**1**

Place card along bottom edge of your envelope paper and trace around card.

**2**

Fold paper at top of card outline.

**3**

Cut along the fold line just to the traced card outline. Fold edges in.

**4**

Cut off excess edges along the sides of the top half.

**5**

Round top corners of envelope flap and fold down.

**6**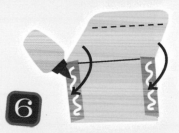

Glue side-flap edges to top flap to close.

# JUST RELaX...

**You'll want to create personal images** and greetings for your cards that reflect ideas and feelings that you'd like to share.

Tap into those feelings by relaxing. Sit in a cozy chair or lie in a comfortable quiet spot. Breathe deeply and slowly for a few minutes. Close your eyes and try to just focus on your breathing.

Now imagine you are in a beautiful and relaxing place. You might picture yourself sitting on a sandy beach, or in front of a campfire, or walking in a large open field. Perhaps you're looking into the sky on a beautiful, warm summer day or taking a warm bath by candlelight. Notice the details around you using each of your senses. What images and colors do you see? What are you thinking? What do you hear and smell? How are you feeling?

When you are done, slowly open your eyes and notice how relaxed you are. Draw and write about your relaxation place in a journal or on a piece of paper. Use some of these images and ideas to make your greeting cards special.

**1** Use markers to draw images from your relaxation place.

**2** Spray lightly over picture so that a fine mist of water lands on the paper.

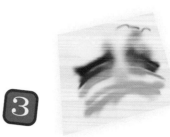

**3** Watch your lines blossom into lovely, misty designs. Your picture will take on a dreamy look. Let dry (you can speed up the drying process with a hair dryer, if desired).

## You'll Need
- white paper
- waterbased markers
- spray bottle of water
- hair dryer (optional)

## Girl Talk

"My relaxation place is a quiet spot in the woods near where I live. It's very peaceful among the trees, ferns, and mosses there. When I look up I can see the sky through a roof of green leaves. It's very private. Only my closest friends and some birds, butterflies, and a little squirrel know about it." Tori

**4** Frame parts of the image you like with paper strips.

**5** Cut or tear out these sections.

**6** Glue in place on the front of your card.

# CARD COLLECTION

**There are many ways to create** awesome cards. Combine the icons on the opposite page with symbols and colors shown on pages 46–49. Cut shapes out of colored paper, clip magazine pictures and text, and use photos and found objects. Arrange them on the front of your card. When you are pleased with the balance of your design, use a few drops of white glue (the kind that dries clear) to fasten each piece.

Girl Talk

"Never feel that you have to compromise your values for someone else. Be who

54

To remind you of all the beauty and wonder in the world.

To heal hurt feelings in your friends and yourself.

To remind you how sweet friendship is.

To remind you to eat right.

To remind you to like yourself when you look in the mirror.

To remind you that you shine.

To remind you to look for the silver lining in every cloud.

To remind you that it's OK to make a mistake.

To remind you to do at least one thing that you feel good about every day.

To remind you that friends can be counted on.

To remind you that friendship ties our hearts together.

To remind you to stay flexible.

you are, and if someone doesn't like it, she's not really your friend." Caitlin

# MAGNIFICENT MESSAGES

**Let people who are special to you** know how you feel about them by writing them a special message. You can put it in a card you've made—and add one of your homemade spa creations from the recipes in this book.

Begin by thinking of things you'd like to say to your friends and family members. Jot down some of the special qualities you see in them, and add a few thoughts that describe how you feel about them.

**1** Practice writing message on a scrap of paper. Space the letters and words so they look balanced on your paper.

**2** Lightly write the message on your card in pencil.

**3** Write the message in pen or colored pencil, using the light pencil lines as a guide.

**4** If you've written the message on a separate piece of paper, glue it into the inside of your card.

I am alone, come be with me.
Open my eyes, help me to see.
I am sad, wipe my tears.
I am glad, join my cheers.
Thank you for being my friend.
Megan

MOM
I respect and admire you.
You are always there for me
when I need you.
I love you.
Bobbi

You listen to me.
You are my friend
in good times and
in bad times.
Tabatha

# Girl Talk

"Family means unconditional love and support. They are a lot like your friends except they're related. They hold the same qualities, yet they never ever leave your side." Salima

My family,
you are
neverending
love,
support,
and a
source of
strength.
Jessica

Family is very, very important to me. It reminds me that there is no place like home. I am lucky to have you. I love all the fun times we have together.
Tori

A friend is somebody that I can be truthful, honest, and kind to. It's somebody like you...somebody I can just plain have fun with, and somebody I want to hang out with...somebody that I can just be myself with.

Sarah

## That Makes Scents!

Make yourself feel great by doing something special for someone—and don't tell the person what you did!

# GIFT BOXES & BASKETS

**Delight your family and friends** with a homemade set of your sweet-smelling creations. You can easily put together a perfect present for a birthday, holiday, or special occasion. Personalize the packages by putting together products in the favorite color and scent of the person receiving the gift. Add colored labels and designs that reflect your relationship. The thought and time that you invest will make your gift even more special.

Package your creations in a fancy basket or box. Whether you buy new or recycle one that you already have, personalize your package. If you choose a basket, wrap ribbon or raffia around the handle and weave it in and out of the sides. Or transform an ordinary shoebox into a treasured gift by gluing on photos and bits of brightly colored paper.

Fill any empty spaces in your gift basket with scrunched up tissue paper or bubble wrap. And complete your gift with a bow and a card (see pages 50–57 for ideas for making your own cards).

If you like, you can use a large piece of clear plastic to wrap your entire gift package. Plastic gift wrap can be found in stores that sell wrapping paper. Simply place your package in the center of the plastic wrap, pull up all the edges, gather, and tie with a ribbon.

**That Makes**

A kind word, thought, or attitude can be a wonderful gift. Positive thoughts make you feel good about yourself, and can make the people around you feel better as well.

**Scents!**

# Girl Talk

"Being around friends and family makes me feel good about myself. No matter what, they comfort me with the gift of compliments. People who make me feel bad about myself only see what's on the outside. I realize that the people who care about me take the time to get to know me and see what's inside of me." Janelle

# YOUR GIFTS

## Be proud of your talents.

Recognize and celebrate the person you are by taking the time to care for your unique body, mind, and spirit. And be generous in sharing those gifts with others. Surround yourself with people who support you and encourage you to be the best version of you, and do the same for them.

Thank your true friends and supportive family for just being themselves! A wonderful way to do that is to put together a gift basket of homemade spa goodies that you've made especially for them.

"Surround yourself with people who respect you. It is not worth trying to change yourself to be popular. Be who you want to be, and want to be who you are, because that is just what you were meant to be, and you're great!" Natalie

Your life is a gift. Enjoy it. Take care.

# MORE ON
# GIRLS' SPA

## Recommended books & websites

*Art for the Heart:*
*Creative Art Expression for You*
*and Your Friends*

**By Mary Wallace**
**Maple Tree Press (2002)**

*Body Talk:*
*The Straight Facts on Fitness, Nutrition,*
*and Feeling Great About Yourself*

**By Ann Douglas and Julie Douglas**
**Maple Tree Press (2002)**

*The Girls' Book of Wisdom:*
*Empowering, Inspirational Quotes*
*from over 400 Fabulous Females*

**By Catherine Dee (editor)**
**Warner Books (1999)**

*Home Made Best Made:*
*Hundreds of Ways to Make all Kinds*
*of Useful Things*

**The Reader's Digest Association, Inc. (1998)**

*Natural Beauty at Home:*
*More than 200 Easy to Use Recipes*
*for Body, Bath and Hair*

**By Janice Cox (editor)**
**Henry Holt Company (1995)**

## Girls Inc.
**An inspiring site that encourages girls**
**to be strong, smart, and bold**
http://www.girlsinc.org

## Girl Power
**Positive health messages for girls 9 to 14**
**by the U.S. Department of Health and**
**Human Services**
http://www.girlpower.gov

## A Girl's World
**A website for young teens that features**
**advice, pen pals, chat, diaries, current**
**events, book and movie reviews**
http://www.agirlsworld.com

## Kitchen Cosmetics
**Homemade natural bath and beauty recipes**
http://www.geocities.com/Heartland/Prairie/8088/
beauty.html

## Make-Stuff.com
**Formulas for making your own health**
**and beauty products**
http://www.makestuff.com/formulas/index.html

## Sunshinecity Soapworks
**Simple recipes for bath products**
http://www.suncitysoap.com/bathtime.html

# Special thanks
## to the girls who contributed to this book:

Tabatha Anderson
Amanda Butler
Caitlin Caldwell
Victoria Casier
Bethany Chandler
Bobbi Cowan
Erin Craig
Janelle Craig
Christine Dewancker
Jenny Dieleman
Tallie Westel
Erin Intven
Kate Intven
Katherine Intven
Meg Intven
Natalie Intven
Tess Intven
Salima Kanami
Amber Laken
Elizabeth McLaws
Jessica Monk
Joan Somers
Rebecca Wallace
Sarah Westaway
Jan Neville

# Index

allergies
  avoid allergic reactions 9
  test patches 9
  nut allergy 8, 13, 18, 28,
    30, 34, 40
Asia 15

bath
  bath sizzlers 18
  bath soaking salts 16
  bubble bath 20
  scented bath powder 26
beauty 4, 6, 45
body art 14

candles 42
cards
  card covers 52–55
  create a card 50
  messages and greetings
    55–57
color 12, 48
  meaning of 7, 48
  mixing 12
communication 30, 48
containers 11
cosmetics 11

Egyptians (Ancient) 50

family 56, 57, 58, 59, 60
feet
  anatomy 41
  foot scrub 40
  foot soak 16
fingerprints 7
fragrance 13
  scented sachets 13
friendship 32, 41, 50, 56,
  57, 58, 59, 60, 61

gifts
  boxes and baskets 58
  candles of light 42
  your gifts 60
Greeks (Ancient) 18

health and well being 48
  attitude 26, 27, 30, 57, 58
  breathing exercises 21
  stress (coping) 4, 19, 24
  stretching exercises 23
  your relaxation place 52–53
hair
  herbal hair rinse 36
  growth rate 35
  natural style 37
  shampoo 34
hands 32, 47
  fingerprints 7
  hand cream 32–33
henna (also mehndi) 14–15
herbs 13, 36

ingredients 8–9
Inuit igloo 42

Keller, Helen 29

labels 44

mehndi *see* henna

Persian brides 15
personality
  optimism 27
  your unique spark 4, 6
personal logo 6

recipes
  bath powder 26
  bath sizzlers 18
  bath soaking salts 16
  body art 14
  body lotion 28
  body scrub 24
  bubble bath 20
  candles 42
  foaming face wash 38
  foot scrub 40
  hand cream 32
  herbal hair rinse 36
  lip gloss 30
  shampoo 34
  shower gel 22
role model 29
Romans (Ancient) 11

scrubbing sponge 25
senses
  smell 13
skin care (face & body)
  body lotion 28
  body scrub 24
  cucumber (for eyes) 38
  foaming face wash 38
  hand cream 32
  lip gloss 30
  shower gel 22
symbols 6–7, 42, 46–47, 55

tools 10

vanilla plant 13

water (beliefs) 17, 18